MW00412474

Parent Chat

Parent Chat

THE TECHNOLOGY TALK FOR EVERY FAMILY

Matt McKee

I dedicate this book and journey to my wife, Jessica, and my two sons, Patriot and Azlan.

I also want to thank Aspen Grove, Kathy Hill, and Adam Duckworth for making this project a reality.

Contents

Introduction - Why Parent Chat?

What Is Happening?   21

22

1 Big Picture of Technology

2 Personal Picture of Technology   32

What Can I Say?   39
Relational Solutions

3 The Right Questions To Ask When   40
    Adding Technology
4 Conversations and Modelling   48
5 Good Conversations Start with   56
    Good Questions

What Can I Do?   63
Technical Solutions

6 Limits   64

7 Passwords are Doorways   74

8 What Can I Do with the New...   82

9 Put out a BOLO   92

Conclusion   98

Introduction

Why Parent Chat?

Fear or Ignorance...or Both...

Most parents I know feel one of two ways about technology when it comes to their children. They are afraid of technology and the damage it could cause, or they are ignorant of technology and don't know what it can do or what they can do about it. Parents I know also feel like they are always behind. Even if they have all the latest gadgets and software, they live in uncertainty — fearing that the next technological gizmo will make them irrelevant as parents.

Irrelevance is scary

Feeling like you are irrelevant as a parent is a strong feeling. It's not just a feeling of being uncool or left out. That is a part of it; no one wants to be the uncool parent. The more painful part of irrelevance, however, is that your relationship with your children seems stripped of purpose. Being irrelevant to your children means being unable to influence or guide them. And that is scary. I know, because I have felt that way myself.

"Dad, I don't want other kids to see what I've seen."

The events that led to me hearing my son say, "Dad, I don't want other kids to see what I've seen," started with my nine year old son, spending the night with some buddies.

While at a friend's house, my son and his friends found a new piece of technology to explore—an iPad©. They started playing, exploring, searching, and eventually, their curiosity led them to content that no nine year old should see. Not long after that, I started to notice some things. My son's behavior changed. He was just basically acting "weird." My dad-radar was going off, and I knew there was something wrong.

I needed to know what was happening, so I started by asking him a question. But I didn't ask him something that would make him defensive, like "What's wrong with you?" I didn't want him to shut down and shut me out. I wanted him to open up so that I could find out about what was going on in his world.

I asked, "What have you seen recently that bugged you or was interesting to you?" The answer I got back shocked me and broke my heart.

"Dad, Superman and Wonderwoman take off their clothes sometimes."

In time, through more conversation, I would discover that it wasn't just one image or one time that something like this happened. There were multiple times when he, either through friends or online predators, was exposed to adult content.

Before I tell you the rest of the story about what happened with my son, let's talk about adult content. It's likely a reason you picked up this book and is the type of content that most scares parents—and for good reason. Mature sexual content is a massive problem in our world. Developmental experts are now saying that an entire generation of young men may be permanently sexually damaged by their constant exposure to it,[1] and girls are equally damaged and victimized.[2] Most experts claim the driving force of this generational damage is a shift, empowered by mobile technology, toward constant, unfettered access and availability.

When you and I grew up, mature content was more easily limited by physical and financial barriers. When I was exposed to it, it was contained in a physical place—a magazine—that was hidden in a physical location—a family member's house. I had limited access to that location and no ability to purchase a similar magazine for myself.

Today, adult content doesn't stay hidden under the bed at an uncle's house across town. It can be accessed from any innocuous-seeming device with an Internet connection—at a friend's house, on the bus, in your living room, or in the back of your car. The content that exists today is also more extreme, more addicting, and contains not just nudity or sexual content, but strong themes of violence, rape, misogyny, and torture.

My friend, Jason Tilley, is a pastor and a co-founder of Aspen Grove—a firm helping families and churches to address living in an increasingly digital world. Long ago, Jason noticed that the Motion Picture Association of America's© (MPAA) rating system for movies (G, PG, PG13, R, NC17) and the Entertainment Software Rating Board's© (ERSB) rating system for video games (C, E, T, M, A) didn't have a rating that truly described some content. Some content is, as Jason put it, "Not suitable for anyone under the age of death." And he is right—there is stuff out there that no one

1 http://time.com/4277510/porn-and-the-threat-to-virility/

2 http://time.com/4277523/girls-sex-women-porn/?iid=toc_033116

needs to see, and your children can just stumble across it. If you think too much about the easy availability of this visual poison, you can be paralyzed with fear. I know that feeling.

In the moment I discovered what my son had been exposed to, I felt irrelevant. I felt like a failure. I wanted to be a good influence on my son and to shape his view of the world in a positive way, and yet, at a vulnerable time in his development, he was victimized. Not long after that, as a dad, I listened to my nine year old son tell me, "Dad, I don't know if I can handle this anymore."

As a parent, that made me angry — not because I thought my son was bad but because I could see how he was victimized by those who took advantage of his simple curiosity. I was angry because I want my children to be curious and to explore, but I also want them to be safe.

This wasn't a nine-year-old's problem.
It was a problem for our whole family.

To address this problem, our entire family had to have a conversation and go on a journey together — learning how to live with technology. This book is about inviting you to the conversation our family went through. You will discover, as we did, that access to mature sexual content is only a small part of a huge problem that we all face.

In the process, we learned some things about technology, but we learned more about ourselves. We learned that all of us were addicted to technology. It was hard to put down devices and look at each other. It was hard to disconnect from the Internet and talk to each other. *This wasn't a nine-year-old's problem. It was a problem for our entire family.*

And we dealt with it as a family. We all had to get involved and discuss the expectations, the purpose of, and use of technology as a part of our family. That discussion went far beyond what type of content a child might be able to stumble across and it led us to realize that we all needed to change the way we used technology. We needed to put limits on what we did in our home. When, where, and for how long we used devices—it all needed to change. Our discussion and the struggle to make these changes was the beginning of creating this resource, *Parent Chat*, and being involved in Circle© with Disney©.

From Victim to Advocate

More importantly to me, however, was how our family's journey led my son from being victimized to being active in helping others avoid what happened to him. His words to me, "Dad, I don't want other kids to see what I've seen" led to him becoming an advocate for other children. It eventually led to a meeting with the technology director at his school, where he delivered a Circle with Disney device to help keep children at his school safe.

There is Hope

I share this story about my family because I imagine that, more than likely, if you are picking up this book, something bad has already happened. If so, you are in the same place I was.

I'm here to tell you that there is hope. Nothing is broken that can't be fixed. My son's story, my family's story, is here to tell you that you and your family members don't have to be victims. Taking control of our family's technology and refocusing our family on relationships was something our family desperately needed, but we might never have done it without discovering what happened to my son. What was broken about our family wasn't that my son saw some adult content. That was just a warning sign. What was broken about us was our addiction to technology.

I thought the worst thing that could have happened was my son's exposure to adult content, but I found out that wasn't true. The worst thing that could have happened was if our family had stayed the same—addicted to technology, consumed by gadgets, and isolated from each other in our own home.

The world has always been a dangerous place for children. There has never been a time when families have been immune from or unable to be touched by darkness and evil in many forms. Our family realized that the same thing that sustained families generations ago through challenges and difficulty is still available. Relationships, conversation, love, guidance, learning, and forgiveness are tools that can both protect your family from such dangers and help your family recover when, despite your best plans and practices, something bad slips through or is stumbled upon out in the world.

You are THE un-hackable "parental control"...

Some parts of this book are about technical solutions for things—which button to press, which setting to adjust, what device to install, what apps to avoid—but those technical precautions are all defeatable with enough ingenuity and determination.

The number one un-hackable setting you need to adjust, the number one "parental control" you are going to discover, is you, the parent. There is no technology that can do what you can do. No screen can hug them like you can. No app can love them like you can. No chat room can share their heartaches like you can. No video game achievement can please them like your cheers and your enthusiastic pat on the back. You are THE "parental control" in their lives.

A conversation starts with questions.

This book is structured around three questions regarding technology that we need to discuss.

What is happening?

This section discusses the history and progress of technology—how it is different now, and how it is changing moving forward.

What can I say?

This section covers what you can do relationally by asking questions, having conversations, and focusing your home on relationships, not on technology.

What can I do?

This section covers what you can do technically by setting different kinds of limits and by understanding settings, devices, and apps.

As we discuss these three questions you will learn to unlock your power to influence your child and train them to navigate this dangerous world, including the dangers of technology.

Let's get started by taking a big picture, wide angle view of where technology comes from and where it is going.

Question 1

What is happening?

Any sufficiently advanced technology is
indistinguishable from magic. — Arthur C. Clarke

Chapter 1

The Big Picture of Technology
The Stuff of our Dreams and our Nightmares

It's amazing how scientific development follows the path laid out by our fictional dreams of both the distant and near future. Jules Verne's novel, From the Earth to the Moon, was published in 1865. In 1902, it inspired the first science fiction film, Georges Méliès' A Trip To The Moon. Then, only 104 years after Verne's novel, we made the fantasy real with the Apollo moon landing. NASA even chose a similar launch location as in the fictional Verne story. Kennedy Space Center was built on the eastern coast of Florida while Jules Verne had described the giant gun to fire his protagonists to the moon being built on the western coast of Florida. Science fiction hasn't just inspired new realities in huge, space-exploring, government agencies. It inspired the men and women who built the devices and technologies that now fill our homes.

The dreams...

So much of today's technology is like wish-fulfillment of the gadgets we loved from science fiction movies and television shows we grew up watching. Our science fiction heroes took us into their homes, businesses, and secret hide-outs that were full of wonderful, imaginative technology that we wished and hoped would be in our homes soon. And now, many of those dreams have, indeed, become part of our lives and our homes.

Star Trek® communicators became flip phones, and now, our smart phones are practically tri-corders. We use them to explore our world as they feed us all kinds of location based information, and even take read-outs from health management devices that monitor our sleep patterns, activity levels, and pulse rates.

Ever since Dick Tracy® did it, we've been wanting to chat with people on our watches. Thanks to Apple Watch® and others we finally can.

Siri® from Apple®, Cortana® from Microsoft®, and Alexa® from Amazon® might not be quite as slick as the computer from Star Trek or Jarvis® from Iron Man®, nor as loveable as C-3PO® or R2-D2®, but smart, robotically voiced assistants that understand you, answer you, and find you information you need are here to stay and they are getting smarter and better every year.

The Jetson's® flat screen television became, well, flat screen televisions. And they are getting even thinner every year. The Jetson's robotic vacuum cleaner became the Roomba®. Also, remember when the Jetsons would push a button and the food or product they wanted would show up at their house? Amazon now has "Dash Buttons™" that you can put in the places where you store commonly purchased items such as laundry detergent or mac and cheese. Just push the Dash Button for that specific item, and Amazon will send it to your house. In many places, the delivery will even be on the same day.

The nightmares...

The dreams of science fiction aren't the only things we have brought to life with technology. Some of the horrible threats to humanity imagined in science fiction have also become real threats that we are currently navigating.

The corruption of reality television, the effects of environmental pollution on the poor, and the method of terrorism used by the 9/11 hijackers were all predicted by Stephen King's novella, *The Running Man*.

No one has yet created a rampaging herd of raptors, but scientists are currently pursuing many of the cloning techniques forecast in Michael Crichton's *Jurassic Park*.

The global problems of inequality and inequity explored in the 1927 film *Metropolis* and in *The Time Machine* by H. G. Wells are part of our current political struggles.

The security of information and free speech are very much under threat today, bringing the fictional worlds from George Orwell's *1984*, and Ray Bradbury's *Fahrenheit 451* frighteningly close to reality.

Why is this important?

Technology isn't just some magical solution to our problems. It also isn't some soulless evil, that has come to destroy us. Both the world of dreams and the world of terrors are made possible by technology. That is because technology is just an extension of our nature — a result of our efforts to solve the problems we encounter in life. Technology penetrates our lives and culture, not because it is part of an evil plot, but because it is answering problems that we struggle with every day.

Think about the technology you use each day when you leave your house, the problems those technologies help you solve, and how that technology has changed.

From two pockets to three pockets.

I used to pat two pockets when I left the house—checking that I had my wallet and keys with me. Now I pat three pockets. You probably do the same thing. Why? Because we added a third "thing" that is a vital part of our life. Our phones, our technology, have now become as vital to us as our wallet and keys. These items each represent an area of our world that we need to have access to in daily life.

- ☐ Wallet = Economic Access—Your wallet gives you access to the economy. Everywhere you go, you carry identification and the means to purchase goods and services.

- ☐ Keys = Physical Access—Whether it is shelter (your home), belongings (storage), or transportation (vehicle), you carry with you the means to access the places you go and your means to get there.

- ☐ Phone/Device = Relationship and Information Access—Our devices connect us to any person and any piece of information we need, at any time that we need it.

The phone as the third "thing" we carry is not the result of some new-fangled whim but of a desire for connection to knowledge and relationships that humans have always had. We have always wanted communication and information at our fingertips. It's why we created writing, the printing press, books, and libraries. It's why there used to be a pay phone on almost every corner. It's why we were once able to call any business, restaurant, hotel, or airport and leave a message for someone or even have them paged to come to a wired "courtesy phone" for calls. It is why we relied on physical messenger services to carry vital, daily business communication. The desire to be always connected and to have constant access to people and information is not new. It's just that we now have technology that makes it possible.

Soon you will be patting two pockets again, then only one pocket...

The days of patting three pockets on the way out the door are...on the way out the door. Our devices are in the process of absorbing the capability of economic access. You can go almost anywhere now and pay with your phone using one of many methods. The wallet is going digital.

Physical access isn't that far behind. There are already doors and locks that can be opened by your phone or other device without needing a key. To open our front doors with our phones, all you and I have to do is pay for and install the new hardware—the new doors or door knobs.

Every "thing" we've always wanted...

But it isn't just your daily carry items that are changing. Every "thing" in your home will soon be a part of a network of data-gathering, recording, reporting, interconnected devices. If you haven't heard the term, "The Internet of Things" is becoming a reality. More and more common household items, articles of clothing, and appliances are going to start having features that utilize Internet connectivity in some way.

All of these items are amazing and have the ability to help us organize and control our lives in ways we could not do just a few years ago. They are, quite literally, the products of our imaginations made real. But these things also bring with them dangers. How do we deal with our simultaneous attraction to, and fear of, technology? How do we separate the dreams from the nightmares?

What should our response be?

There are at least three paths we can take.

The Path of Acceptance

The path of acceptance is the path I see the majority of families on. On this path, we try everything right out of the box. We become early-and-often adopters. We stand in line for the newest tech. We *never* read the End User License Agreements — we just click accept. We jump in and go along with all the latest trends, tech, and culture. We don't worry, we just enjoy the ride and hope nothing goes wrong.

The problem with this path is that it puts too much trust in technology, culture, and the government that regulates them to keep us safe. Governments don't move quickly and technology does. Regulation takes years, decades even. Think about how many people had to die before the government starting forcing us to wear seatbelts. The path of acceptance is a fun ride, but it can end in tragedy.

The Path of Rejection

On the path of rejection, we reject dangerous, cutting-edge technology. We withdraw from the new. We have a "dumb" phone (and are, sometimes, puritanically proud of the fact). We do not participate in new devices, communication methods, or the culture that they create and support.

There's an entire culture here in the USA that decided a long time ago to opt out of further technology. They didn't do it out of fear but out of a desire for simplicity. They drew the line at zippers and horseless carriages.

> *Zippers? That's too much technology. Buttons are the most advanced clothing technology we need.*

> *Horseless carriages? Nope. Horses and buggies can take me anywhere I need to go, thank you very much. If my horse and buggy can't get me there, maybe God doesn't want me to go.*

And, do you know what? They are exactly right. You don't *need* zippers. You don't *need* trucks or cars. You don't *need* mobile devices or computers. This is a perfectly valid choice you can make about technology and culture, but you can probably tell I wouldn't make that choice and I don't think you or your children would either.

Here's why I don't make this choice: I'm less worried about me and my children being influenced by the culture than I am about me and my children not having a voice in the culture around us.

You can drive up to the countryside in Pennsylvania and buy some fantastic furniture or quilts from people who only travel in horse drawn buggies. We could and should learn a lot from these communities about sustainability and stewardship of resources. They have a lot to teach us about the benefits of quietness, of meditation, of humility, and of living simply.

However, you won't find these communities having a huge effect on culture outside of their immediate surroundings. That is because radically withdrawing from technology means radically withdrawing from culture, and it is difficult to have a voice in a culture you have radically withdrawn.

The Path of Relationship

On the path of relationship, we enter the world of new technology with care, with mindfulness, and with an intentional, relationship-centered purpose. With new technologies we go slowly and test carefully. We allow our relationships to give purpose to our technology usage and never let technology disrupt the purpose of our relationships. On this path, our relationships can benefit from the power of technology instead of being wrecked by it, and through our relationships outside the family, we have a voice in the culture of our friends, our schools, our communities, and, ultimately, the world.

This is the path I hope to help you and your family choose by reading this book.

Technology is not the hero of our dreams or the villain of our nightmares.

Technology is not the problem. We are. Technology is amoral—neutral. But technology is also a mirror. The story of technology, both the good and the bad, is a story about us. But, when we look in the mirror of technology, we don't just see how it changed the world, we see how it changed us. We are different because of the way technology has developed. As it changed, it changed us, too.

In the next section, we will look at the personal picture of technology—how it has changed in your life and why your life and your children's lives are completely different because of the effects of technology.

Chapter 2

The Personal Picture of Technology
What has Changed and What Hasn't

Technology has changed a lot over time and, as it changed, we changed with it. We are different from our parents partly because of the effects of technology, and the same is true for our children.

Remember the time...

Adults and children perceive time differently. The years just seem to go by more quickly to us, don't they? To children, however, time doesn't move at all or seems to crawl imperceptibly. We feel rushed and anxious, while they feel trapped and bored. We lean back, wanting to slow down because we feel we are speeding faster and faster, while they lean forward, longing to push ahead into a future that can't get here fast enough.

If you have children, all it takes is looking back at your first pictures of them, for you to realize how quickly they grow and how quickly time seems to be passing. We think to ourselves, "Where did that time go?" Years seem to pass like weeks or days. But to your children, those years took... years! And if you ask them about it, the weeks took years too! Time moves slowly from their perspective.

Partly because of the way we feel that yesteryear was yesterday, we make two key mistakes when we think about our children.
1. We think our children are just like we were.
2. We think they are growing up like we grew up.

In our minds, we think we aren't that different from our children. Because our younger selves seem so close in our memories, we think that we know what our children are like because we know what we were like.

However, they are very different from us because the world they were born into is so very different from the world we were born into.

Here's some perspective for you. Start by thinking of your child's birthdate. Got that date fixed in your mind? I'm going to list some events and dates. You just think one of two words after each date: "before" if your child was born before the date, or "after" if your child was born after the date.

- ☐ The first televised advertisement featuring the first iPhone™ was broadcast during the 79th Academy Awards in February of 2007. To remind you how long ago that was, *Happy Feet, Cars, and Monster House* were nominated for Best Animated Feature. (*Cars* should have won.) *An Inconvenient Truth* won Best Documentary and *The Departed* won best picture.
- ☐ The first iPhones were sold on June 29th of 2007[3].
- ☐ The Apple App Store debuted on July 10th of 2008.
- ☐ *Angry Birds* was originally released for Apple iOS in December of 2009.

How many times did you think "before"? I'm guessing not very many. I don't know when you are reading this book, but at the date of my writing it, in early 2016, any child younger than nine has never lived in a world that didn't have iPhones in it. Just think for a minute about life in the "pre-iPhone" days.

Before that advertisement on the Academy Awards, most people saw no need for a "smart" phone. Sure, business people had Blackberry™ phones but, for average people, it

---

3 http://www.wired.com/2009/06/dayintech_0629/

was not seen as something they needed. But, when iPhone came on people's televisions and said "hello," the way we thought about phones began to change.

Think of all the things you do with your phone that you used to do in other ways. Your phone is probably within reach as you read this book — or you are actually reading this book on your phone. Think of all the things you can do right now on your phone. Before your children were born, many of the tasks you just thought of would require getting up, perhaps leaving the house, or using multiple forms of technology. Now, the power to do all of those things is right beside you. And your children have never known anything different.

By comparison, if you were born in the 1970's, you were born in the decade that pocket calculators first became available. You have never lived in a world in which you couldn't carry a calculator in your pocket. That was a big deal then. In the 1970's, a computer as powerful as the iPhone was the size of a house or barn. Obviously, technology has greatly developed since we were young, but it isn't just about the amount of technological change. It is the pace. Today, technology is changing, in some ways, exponentially faster.

I happened to be born in what was called the "gap" generation. We were after Generation X, but weren't yet Generation Y. We were in transition. I learned to type on a typewriter. Just four years later, I was learning programming in a computer lab and dying of dysentery as I made yet another attempt on *Oregon Trail*. In just four years, a massive shift happened, and the technology I had just learned how to use was already obsolete. Around the same time, when a friend of mine started college, it was really weird (even for an engineering major) that one of his first roommates had a personal computer in the dorm room. But by the time my friend's younger brother came along just 5 years later, it was nearly unthinkable that any college student could get by without a personal computer. That's some pretty fast technological and cultural change.

Today the rate at which technology advances is even faster. Every year, we get new devices with powerful new capabilities (or improvements on the abilities they had previously). Whatever new technology your children learn this year, will be replaced or outdated next year. Something new and relatively unknown today, in six months might be dominating the market and the world, and in six more months, completely disappear.

You might be thinking right now, "This is terrible! I can't keep up! I might as well give up!" But hold on. That's not true. Let me tell you the good part.

The more people interact with screens or technology, the more people crave real, face-to-face relationships.

That's right. The more we use technology, the more we want real, human interaction.

Technology has radically changed our world and it won't stop changing it. Technology has changed the way we think, the way we learn, the way we work, and the way we socialize. Your children don't do any of those things in the same way that you did. You are different from your children. But that doesn't mean you can't communicate. It doesn't mean technology wins. Parents win. Because parents can do something that technology can't. You can have a relationship.

Parents and children still form memories around real things in their lives. No one says, "Remember that time I posted that picture on Facebook?" Memories are built around real events with real people in the real world.

- ☐ When you had an important conversation...
- ☐ When you first met someone...
- ☐ When you went on a special trip...

Even when we do remember an event that involves technology, we remember it because of the relationships involved, not because of the technology.

- ☐ When we remember that one photo on Facebook that got a bunch of great comments, we remember the moment the photo was taken, the other people in the photo, the person who took the photo, and the people who commented. We don't remember the phone that took it.
- ☐ When your children remember a great moment in an online game they play with their friends, it isn't the game that's important, or the game system. It's their friends.

Relationship trumps technology because technology amplifies our longing for relationship. We just need to make sure that when our children long for relationships, that they know how to have one. Our biggest opportunities with our children have nothing to do with technology. They have to do with being with them in the important moments of life and having conversations about things that matter to them. Children aren't going to look back and say, "remember when" about technology. But they will say, "Remember when you were there for me?" "Remember when we did that thing together?" "Remember when you helped me not to be scared?" "Remember when you encouraged me after I failed?" "Remember when we celebrated?"

For them to say "remember when" about you, there needs to be a "when" that you were there. As the time races by you, are you making time to be present in the moments that matter for your children? Remember, you feel time passing quickly, they feel it passing slowly. When you say, either with your words or your actions, that you don't have time for them, part of the reason they don't understand is because to them, time is slow and all they have is time.

Technology can do some amazing things for your children, and your children will use technology to do some things that will amaze you. But technology can't do for your children what you can do — have a real relationship with them.

What is happening with technology doesn't have to determine what happens in our families. There are relational and technological ways to address this problem. In the next section we will look at shaping our use of technology using relational solutions that are based in questions and conversations. After all, relationships are built around conversations, and conversations start with questions. The first conversation and the first questions we need to ask are about the purpose and power of the technology that we are considering bringing into our homes and our lives.

Question 2

What can I say? - Relational Solutions

"Now we all need to focus on the many, many ways technology can lead us back to our real lives, our own bodies, our own communities, our own politics, our own planet." - Sherry Turkle

Chapter 3

The Right Questions to Ask When Adding Technology

We add technology to our homes often. We do it by adding new hardware, new software, or new users.

New Hardware

The most obvious way is when we add new hardware— when we buy a completely new device that we have never had before. Examples of this may be an iPad, a Kindle™, an additional phone (for a new user like a teenager), an Apple TV™, a Chromecast™, or some other web-connected device that is new to you or your family.

We also add new hardware when we buy or replace familiar piece of hardware with a new version that has new features. An example of this would be buying a new television that connects directly to your home's WiFi and has a built in web browser, or a new car that provides its own WiFi hotspot.

New Software

We also add technology when we start using a new app or service that we have never used before, such as Facebook, Instagram, Periscope or any of thousands of games.

New Users

The last way we add technology is when we add users to devices or services that already are in our home. An example of this is when you decide that your 8 year old can use your phone for games. This can also mean when you decide to allow your children to join a social media site like Facebook or Instagram, or you allow them to post YouTube videos of their video game adventures.

Whether we are adding technology by adding devices, software, or users, we should be asking some important questions about that technology. Unfortunately, most adults ask completely different questions about new technology than children do.

Parent's questions...

When adults expand technology, we think about it from an adult viewpoint and we ask adult-type questions. We are concerned with the benefits of the technology and the reasons behind using it. We also care a lot about the technical details of the product.

We have a list of tasks in our heads that we want the device to do for us. We ask whether the device can do those tasks or whether an updated device can do them better than ever before. The most basic adult technology question boils down to, "What will this device do for me?"

Children don't care about that kind of stuff. They aren't seeking tasks, they are seeking freedom. They don't need the device to do anything specific. They are just in awe of what it might do. Children ask a different question. They ask, "What can it do?"

"What will this do *FOR* me?" Versus, "What *CAN* it do?" These questions might seem similar. But they are very different.

"What will this do *FOR* me?" is pragmatic. It has a purpose and an agenda. It is concerned with tasks. It has a list of qualifications in mind. This question leads to comparison with the specs of past products. It leads to thinking about measurable outcomes. It involves estimating the cost versus the benefit. It leads to reading the operating instructions carefully.

"What *CAN* it do?" is creative. This question has no agenda or task list. It doesn't care about the intended purpose. This question leads to finding the limits and pushing the edges but it rarely leads to reading the operating instructions. This question leads to unexpected and surprising uses. The only goal of this question is freedom and exploration.

Because our questions are different, they will drive us to use technology in different ways. Let me give you a couple of examples.

Blocks

When we give young children blocks, they play with them. They stack them, they arrange them by colors, they build towers, they do a lot of things with them.

Adults look at a child building a tower of blocks and try to read things into it.

"Oh, she's so smart."

"She's so creative!"

"She's gonna be an architect."

In fact, that's probably part of why we bought the child blocks in the first place — we are thinking about the blocks from a viewpoint of purpose and goals. We are asking, "What will they do for my child?"

The child just wanted to knock the tower over. The child

doesn't even think or care that it looks like a building. She's just testing and exploring. Soon she will be throwing the blocks across the room or feeding them to the dog or trying to flush them down the toilet. Those are definitely "off-label" uses, and if you weren't prepared for them, they can lead to some household drama or even damage. Why do children do things like that? Simple. They are asking, "What can it do?" not "What will it do for me?"

Children are explorers

When you bring technology into your home, children will view it in the same way as they view the blocks. "What can it do?" They will test it, try it, and discover "off-label" uses for it.

Children are natural born explorers. They might have some specific tasks they want to do, but they won't ever stop being explorers. You shouldn't want your children to stop being curious or pushing the boundaries. But that does mean that you need to be prepared to be an explorer and think like a child again.

Calculators and becoming explorers again...

One piece of good news is that you used to think like a child. And, I have proof.

Before fancy-graphing calculators that children use today, we had plain-old, ordinary, calculators. Our parents bought them for us after asking a "What can it do *for* me" kind of question. They bought them for a purpose — to help us with schoolwork.

But, we asked "What can it do" type of questions. And that is why you and I know that we can type into an old calculator 0.7734, and then hold the calculator upside down to a friend to say "hello." The old digital screens wouldn't show all the letters of the alphabet, but we worked around it. After learning to say, "hello," we discovered many more things we could say—some appropriate, but many inappropriate.

Question: Who would think to turn a calculator screen upside down and see if it could spell words?
Answer: children asking, "What can it do?"

Question: Who would use something intended to do one thing only, math calculations, to communicate with friends?
Answer: children asking, "What can it do?"

Question: Who would think to create an ersatz language with only eight letters that came to be known as "BEGHILOS"?[4]
Answer: children asking, "What can it do?"

You used to be one of those children.

As we bring new technology into our homes we need to ask not just the adult questions but the child questions. We need to open up our minds and become explorers again. We need to be prepared and watch out for "off-label" and unadvertised uses for technology. The most important question to ask when adding new technology to your family's life is, "What can it do?"

---

4   "Words you can write on a calculator - The Guardian." 2014. 2 Feb. 2016 <http://www.theguardian.com/education/datablog/2014/jan/10/words-you-can-write-on-a-calculator>

Once we understand the capabilities of technology we are bringing into our homes, we need to give purpose to it by shaping our family's interactions with it.

In the next chapter we start with you—the parent. There are some specific steps that you as a parent must take to begin shaping and guiding your children's interactions with technology. It starts with conversations and modeling.

Chapter 4

Conversations and Modeling

No app, no device, no anything, can influence your child more than you can. That's good for you! You, the parent, are the primary influence on your child's life.

So, how do you influence your children at home? Two main ways: conversation and modeling.

Conversations lead to discovery

Are you talking to your children regularly? You should be. One of the main ways you influence your children, find out about their world, and discover problems and challenges they face is through conversation.

As parents, we all here technology horror stories. We hear about children pursued by an online stalker. We hear about children emotionally scarred by and addicted to games or inappropriate content. We hear about children getting bullied online or becoming bullies themselves. When I hear these stories, I always ask, "How did you find out about it?" The answer is usually some random occurrence or odd slip-up that tipped off the parent. And, I always reply back with one question. "How often do you just talk to your children?" Having daily conversations with your children—about them, about life, about what is going on in their world—is vital.

Maybe the reason some parents don't know what is going on with their children and technology is that they don't know what is going on with their children at all.

Discover the good

Conversation isn't just how you discover bad things in your children's lives, it is the best way to discover the good things in their lives. Through regular conversation, you will get to know your children. You will learn how they react, how they worry, how they think, how they tell stories, and what kind of relationships are in their lives.

Keys to good conversations

Regularity

The first key to having good conversations with your children is regularity, not rarity. This doesn't mean that conversations must happen at the same time of day or same place every time. It does mean that they should be frequent and free-flowing. These simple interactions will have a much bigger impact than scheduled lectures. Regular conversation is exactly the opposite of "sitting your child down for a talk." We all remember getting "talking-tos" and lectures from parents. They were forced on us. They were one way communication. They felt accusatory. We were uncomfortable. We just wanted them to be over. In contrast, when you fit regular conversations into the flow of life, they feel comfortable, familiar, and it feels normal to share.

The stuff of life

The second key to conversations with your children is to talk about things that are normal in their world. Talk about the stuff of life—the stuff of THEIR lives. When you talk to your children, it's easy to dominate the conversation by telling them what you think they need to know or telling them what to do. Instead, your conversations with them need to be focused on them. Don't talk about whether they completed a task, or a school assignment, or what time an extracurricular activity is, talk about them. Talk about their life not their activities. Talk about their friends not just their classes. Talk about what is happening in their world. Be curious and show interest in them, and you will be surprised how much they open up to you.

Questions, but not interrogation
The third key to conversations with your children is asking questions. It is important to ask questions that require something more than regurgitation of information or yes/no answers. You want to ask open-ended questions that aren't directly aimed at getting any particular kind of information out of them. I will go into more detail about the kinds of questions to ask in the next chapter.

Conversation > Interrogation

If you talk to your children regularly, you won't have to interrogate them about technology or anything else. Things will just come up normally in conversation. If you talk to your children regularly, you won't have to gain their trust for them to share important things with you. You will already have it. Because of your investment of time talking with them about all the things they think are important, it will only be natural for them to bring important questions to you. If you can make conversations a priority in your home, discovering problems or issues with technology will be just a normal part of discovering problems or issues with anything else in your children's lives.

Modeling it

In order to put conversations first in our homes, we will need to start with ourselves because the other way that we influence our children is through modeling. They will do what they see us doing.

How many times have you come home, sat on the couch, and pulled out your phone or device to stare at it? Then, every once in awhile you show your device to your spouse and say, "Didya see this on Facebook?"

Great conversation, right?

Go thoughtfully through these questions and take a look at your own technology usage before you start trying to think about your children's use of technology.

Do you view and interact with multiple devices or screens at once? How many at one time and how often does that happen? Have you been watching sports on TV while looking at your fantasy league on a tablet or laptop, and tweeting about the game, while texting your fantasy league buddies on your phone?

How often, while driving, do you look at texts, email, or social media at stop lights? (Because you would never look while you are driving? Right?)

How often have you been talking to a person face to face and you stopped talking to them and gave your attention to a notification from your phone? How often has that happened when the person you were talking to was your child?

How many times in a day is your phone *not* within arms reach?

When was the last time you sat down for a conversation with a family member and neither of you had a phone or device?

How many times have you made your children wait while you interacted with a screen instead of them?

Why do we expect our children to behave differently around technology than we do? We expect them to put it down, turn it off, pay attention...but we aren't modeling it. We aren't showing them how. Are we really surprised that children who end up walking like us, shrugging their shoulders the same way we do, or liking the same sports team that we like would get addicted to technology the same way we do?

How to start? A conversation.

How can you start modeling a healthy relationship with others and with technology? Start with a conversation with your spouse or a trusted friend. You need to have a conversation about goals. Decide what the goals should be for how often your family sets down the devices, turns off the screens, and makes time for conversation.

The dashboard on a car has a lot of good information about what is happening on your drive. The speedometer tells you how fast you are travelling. The gas gauge tells you how much further you can go. The temperature gauge tells you if the engine temperature is getting into dangerous ranges.
You need to design a dashboard with gauges for technology use in your home. The first gauges you need to design need to be for you and your spouse. The next ones for your whole family, and the last ones for your specific children. What will be on that dashboard, and what you want the needles to read is up to you, but you need to have a conversation, and make a decision to start somewhere.

The Good Week gauge:
What makes a good week?

Here's what my wife and I decided. A good week or a bad week depends on one gauge: how many nights a week I am home, around the dinner table with the children, with all the devices off. If our family achieves that four out of seven nights, it's a good week. Anything less than that— it's a bad week. That's one of our gauges of what a good week is for our family, and maybe it would be a good starting place for your family.

Pick a time, turn off the tech, and talk

Your home might need a different gauge or multiple gauges. You might want more nights per week or fewer. Instead of dinnertime you might want a gauge involving breakfast, or an evening walk, or afternoon tea, or drive time. That's fine! Decide what's best for your family, but you have to have the conversation and set the goal. If you don't have a goal, you'll just drift. And drifting hardly ever leads you to a place you want to be.

Before my family had a conversation about this, I wasn't home very many times a week for dinner. It wasn't good. It needed to change, but it didn't change until we had a goal set down. Now, we are seeing success. Get specific about when, how long, and how many family conversation times you want to have a week. Set the goal, turn off the tech, and start talking.

To start a good conversation, you have to know how. I mentioned earlier that we would discuss questions in the next chapter. That is because the best way to start a conversation is asking a good question.

Chapter 5

"I always figured we would cross that bridge when we got there."

Good Conversations Start With Good Questions

Many parents, myself included, aren't good at asking the right kinds of questions to their children. I know that most of the time, when a parent picks a child up from school, they will ask, "How was your day?" I also know that most of the time, children will answer this in the laziest way possible. They will either say, "fine," "good," "okay," or usually just say "nothing."

It's easy to blame the kids. Sure, they are being lazy. But the problem is often the questions we are asking. As parents, we need to not settle for monotone answers often accompanied by a grunt. We need to start asking better questions, leading questions, questions that cause children to reflect, to think, and hopefully to answer with more than one word. We especially need to do so around technology that we are nervous about or don't quite know our way around yet. Many parents will try to start a conversation with a weak question like, "What are you doing online?" That question is rarely going to net anything other than "nothing."

But don't think this means you should be asking highly specific questions either. Asking specific, pointed questions is great for testing, or for police work, but it's lousy for starting conversations. Instead of asking a direct question demanding a specific answer, you need to use open-ended questions that can be answered from a wide range of a child's experience. Asking open-ended questions will help you discover many new things about your children's lives that you won't learn any other way. The question that helped me discover the situation with my son was an open ended question. If I hadn't discovered what was going on as quickly as I had, much more damage could have been done to my son and my family.

Here are three guidelines for the types of questions you should ask, followed by four questions that should be a part of your regular conversations.

Three Guidelines

Don't ask about technology

You don't have to ask about technology to get answers about technology. Children don't see their digital lives as being separate from their regular lives. When you ask about them talking to their friends, they don't separate talking in-person to their friends, texting their friends, talking to their friends via in-game chat, or talking to their friends via social media. It's all just talking to their friends. What we think of as "real" communication and "digital" communication are all part of one big connected world to them. When you ask an open-ended question, if it relates to a part of their digital world, you'll hear about it.

Ask for their opinion or input, not facts.

If you ask for a fact, once the question is answered, the conversation is over. Asking for your children's opinions leads to further discussion. You want to ask questions that show that you value what your children think. Ask questions that encourage them to evaluate their life and express an opinion, make an evaluation, or give input about it. Then you can talk about why they feel or think that way.

Listen carefully. And ask a follow up question.

Children may seem hesitant at first, but you will be surprised how quickly they will open up to you and how much they will share with you. You need to listen carefully. Listen to them and then ask a follow up question. Follow up questions still need to be open, but should take you deeper into your child's world. Some examples of basic follow up questions are, "What does that mean?", "Why would he do that?", or "How does that work?"

After some practice, you won't have any trouble coming up with great questions and follow up questions to start conversations with your children, but it can be intimidating at first. I have four questions below that I think will provide you some great insight and encourage great conversations for your family. Start with these four questions; then, start editing them, changing them, and coming up with questions of your own.

Four Questions

What have you seen recently that was really interesting?

This is a great question to get an idea of what it is like inside your child's world. What are they looking at? What are they focusing on? What concerns them? What is catching their attention? This question will let you know. Some things will be trivial of course, but sometimes you will be shocked by their insight into the world around them.

What is the craziest thing your friends are doing right now?

When asking this question, it's important to not make it sound accusatory or negative. You want to get positive "crazy" things as well as some boundary pushing ones. The best thing about this question is it focuses attention on their friends. Friendships are becoming more and more important to your kids, talking about them reveals a lot about them. Getting to know your children's friends will show you a picture of the path your child is on. Your children won't mind telling on their friends a little bit. It makes them look good by comparison. Doing so lets them gauge your reaction to how bad something is, without actually doing it. Remember, also, that what their friends are doing now, they will be doing soon, or may already be doing. In any case, this question gives you a window into a vital part of their world, their friends.

What is something that surprised you recently?

Again, the answers to this question could be anything: a video they saw, something a friend said, some disappointment at home or school, or a new website they discovered. Anything surprising is noteworthy in your child's world and is usually something they will want to explore again.

Can you teach me how...?

Children love to show us things. When you allow yourself to be taught by your child, you are seeing them learn to communicate, learn to explain things, and you are learning about areas that are important to them. Children love to show you how smart they are and they enjoy sharing things that excite them. When there is something in your life that your child is passionate about, one of the best things you can do as a parent is ask your child to educate you about their passion.

Good conversations lead to good information

Making conservation a priority in your home won't accomplish much if the conversations don't lead anywhere interesting. To help your conversations engage your children, start with these types of questions. Your goal is to make your children the stars of the conversation. Get them sharing about their world, their friends, their opinions, and their favorite things. The information you gain will be valuable in protecting your family in the realm of technology, but it won't be nearly as valuable as the growing strength of your relationship with your children.

Our children are learning more than we ever have and learning it faster than we ever did. Technology is a huge part of that. The best experiences with technology for me today are when I am sitting with my son learning after asking a "Can you teach me..." kind of question. Those moments are precious to me, and you can have those kinds of moments with your children too. But they'll never come if you don't make time for conversation and learn to ask the right questions.

From relational solutions to technical solutions

The best solutions for helping your children with technology are the ones we have just talked about—the relational solutions. However, there are many technical solutions that can help keep your children safer online. Although technical solutions might involve buttons, settings, passwords, and timers, don't think of them as separate from or operating outside your relationship with your children. These settings, rules, and limits go hand in hand with the focus on relationships you need to build in your home. Ultimately, these technical solutions are simply the more tangible part of the relational solutions.

In the first chapter of this section, we will look at limits that we can and should set for our children and for ourselves.

Question 3

What can I do?—Technical Solutions

I can't drive 55! — Sammy Hagar

Chapter 6

"It's not that I don't want to know, it's that he never expounds on my close-ended questions."

Limits

We are very familiar with living in a world with limits. We have limits all around us. But for now, let's just look at examples of limits in one area—motor vehicles. We have speed limits and limits on the levels of drugs or alcohol that may be in your system when driving. We have seatbelt laws for cars and trucks and helmet laws for motorcycles. We have requirements on the minimum safety features a car must have, on how long children must ride in a car seat, and on how old a person must be to have a driver's permit and a license.

Some limits are debatable. People have been arguing for years about whether higher speed limits have a negative effect on safety. But some limits are there for a very specific and obvious reason—to prevent us from doing something dumb, like not wearing a seatbelt or a helmet, or driving under the influence of drugs and alcohol.

We understand all of these limits in the real, physical world, but somehow when it comes to our children and technology, we don't think about digital safety in the same way as physical safety. We just turn over the keys and say, "have fun." That's not smart. You need to set limits for your family's use of technology.

We all chafe against limits at some point. (Remember the rock anthem of those who learned to drive in the 1980's, *I Can't Drive 55?*) Undoubtedly, as I begin to talk about the kinds of limits I use with my family, you and I will have some points of disagreement. You will begin to chafe and strain at even the thought of some of the limits I will propose. That's okay. Don't throw the book away. Just hear me out and try to tell the difference between the limits that might be debatable and the ones that are intended to keep you from doing something dumb.

Also, remember to look for the purpose behind the limit. If you can make an adjustment to the limit while still accomplishing the purpose for your family, that will be great. But, you need to be open to change and making difficult sacrifices for the long term benefit of your family. You need to discuss limits with your spouse and find a system that you both can agree to enforce. (Notice I didn't say a system your children approve of.)

You wouldn't let your children out on the road driving a powerful vehicle that is capable of killing them or others without giving them some training and guidance. Wrecking a car isn't the only way your children can wreck their lives. The powerful technology that your children have access to in your home is just as capable of wrecking lives as your car is. So, when they protest, remember that the purpose of these limits is guidance, training, and growth. A plan for growth requires an end goal—and it just so happens I have one in mind.

In the back of this book you will find a copy of the Cell Phone Agreement. A copy of it should be filled out and signed by every child seven or older in your home. Go ahead and flip back there, take a look, and then come back here.

As stated at the top of that document, your family's end goal—the purpose for all of these limits and restrictions—is that by the time your children leave your home, they will have *earned* their way to having *no restrictions* on their phone and Internet use. The reality is, they aren't ready for that amount of freedom now. They need you to help them get ready, and these limits are part of how you do that.

Prepare for the excuses

Before we move on, let's talk preemptively about excuses.

You are probably reading this book because you already have children. If you already have children, they probably are used to the rules and limits currently in your home. If so, they probably aren't going to like the changes I'm about to suggest. They don't have to.

When the laws changed in the 80's and 90's requiring children to wear seatbelts, we didn't like it, and we had plenty of excuses as to why we shouldn't obey the new guidelines. But now, most people realize that those laws are just common sense.

Here is the main excuse that you are going to get when you try to limit when and where your children can use devices. "But I need my phone in my room all night! I use it for an alarm clock!" This excuse is classic and follows the format of most excuses your children will try regarding technology.

"I need access to this *harmless, mundane, and ordinary function*, so therefore you must give me *free and uncontrolled access to all the functions of this device* so that I may use this harmless, ordinary, mundane function."

This logic is ridiculous. The devices we own do everything, including mundane tasks like an alarm clock or a calculator or a calendar. But that doesn't mean your children need them to do those tasks. It's simple. Buy a dollar store alarm clock to wake your child up in the morning. He doesn't need 24 hour unlimited access to a powerful mini-computer in order to wake up on time.

I don't know what creative arguments your children will use as excuses, but don't give in. You might even come up with a few excuses of your own for suggestions of limits that you don't like. When you or your children object to some of the suggestions I make, look at the objections carefully and analyze them. If your main argument is on behalf of convenience over safety, you probably are looking at an excuse. Most excuses follow a pattern—they suggest abandoning security and wisdom for a little bit of convenience. Don't derail your plans to keep your children and home safe and secure for minor inconveniences and excuses.

Most of the excuses your children will give as objections to limits aren't anything new. They are the exact same excuses you gave your parents for things in the past.

"But all my friends are..."

"Everyone gets to..."

"Other parents don't..."

If you ask around, you will probably find out that none of that is true. All their friends aren't. Everyone isn't. And the other parents? Most likely, they are struggling just as much as you are. Talk to other parents. You'll probably find out they have the same concerns you do. If possible, work together with other parents to set similar limits and monitor behavior, but don't be pressured by them to cave on the standards you want to set for your family. Remember, you haven't escaped peer pressure just because you aren't in high school anymore. And there is nothing wrong with being the "uncool" mom or "uncool" dad.

Customize your limits

As I talk through the limits, I'll share those that I set for my own children in our home. Your home will be different, so don't feel tied down to my rules. But I hope they will be useful to you as a starting point.

Borders

The first limit involves borders. Borders separate areas from each other. We are familiar with borders between countries, states, and even cities in metro areas. We are also familiar with borders for certain activities. At the park, you can ride your bike on the bike trails, but not on the baseball diamond. Your dog can only be unleashed within the fence of the dog park area. You can smoke in the park, but only in designated smoking areas.

Your home needs borders to designate safe areas for technology to be used by you and by children. As a general rule, this means that no technology will be allowed in a private space. That means no technology should be allowed in bedrooms or any room with a closed door.

In our home, the children's bedrooms are upstairs, so the border is the stairs. No technology goes upstairs for any reason. The phones and devices all must be used in the open, downstairs. They all have a place downstairs out in the open where they go at night and where they charge.

Screen time limits

The use of screens (phones, game systems, televisions, tablets, computers, anything with a screen) needs to be limited by time somehow. There are different ways to do this. You can have a specific time window each day during which technology is not to be used or, reversing that, a time window that is the *only* time technology can be used. You can also have a certain amount of time that the children are freely able to use as they wish at any time during the day. This is a little harder to enforce without some technological help to track the usage, but it is a great system that gives them a little more freedom.

In our home, our children have thirty minutes when they first get home to use technology for homework. Their school uses an online system for them to retrieve and complete assignments on a computer or tablet. Then, for the rest of the evening they have ninety minutes of screen time that they can use whenever they want. During that time, they also have to eat dinner (no screens during that time), do chores, spend some time outdoors, and sometimes other activities. Both individual and family activities count against their time. So if we watch sports, a TV show, or movie as a family, that counts as part of their screen time.

You need limits too

As you impose limits on your children, remember that you need to be modeling how to deal with limits. To do that, they need to see the limits you set affecting what you do. Your limits don't have to be the same as theirs, but they need to be observable by your children in their normal lives. For example, at least part of your "no phone" time, needs to happen before your children go to bed, so they can see you put the phone down and choose to spend time with them. You might need to wear a watch or put clocks around the house so you don't use the excuse of "I need my phone as a timepiece." Your children need to see you getting text messages in the car while driving, but not looking at them or responding. This isn't just about their sense of fairness, it's about training them. You need to model it for them or they won't understand how to do it. If you don't model it, it will be very difficult to get them to stick to the limits you set.

Know your limits—The difference between Tensions and Problems

In our lives, we depend heavily on technology for different things that we do. You may need to stay in touch for work. You may own your own business that requires after hours work. You may have clients (or bosses) who blow up your phone all night long with after hours email questions.

When it is your livelihood that causes a need to stay in touch, it makes it very hard to totally shut things down. These types of adult realities can make for some difficult tensions in our lives, and we need to recognize that. Let your children know what is going on when you wrestle with these things. If work emails or phone calls are interfering with technology down-time with your family, make sure when you step away for an email that must be answered that you don't also glance at Facebook, or send a text message. It's okay to let them see you struggling and fighting to keep technology from intruding on your time.

We will all have tensions that we have to manage moment by moment. Some things, however, aren't tensions. They are problems. Tensions can be managed. Problems need to be solved. When the issue is consistent, and when it starts to damaging how you are connecting with your family and how you are modeling the use of technology to your children, that is an issue that is becoming more than a tension to manage. It's a problem, and you will need to set some kind of limit to solve it.

Problems like this will often come up in an area of weakness for you. I don't know what your weak areas are, but I had a problem with a game.

It started as an attempt to spend more time with my boys. We were playing a cooperative game during their screen time. I thought that it would be cool to play the game with them. I'd be spending time with them. Part of their ninety minutes of screen time would still be "dad time." It was cool for awhile, but after their screen time was up, and they went to bed... I wouldn't stop playing the game. I'd keep playing, racking up achievements and points. Then I'd talk to them later and say, "Did you see the cool thing I did in the game." Their response was grumpy.

"We could if you gave us more screen time." They had a right to be grumpy.

I had taken something we were doing together and allowed it to become something that I did without them for my own enjoyment. In the end, this wasn't a tension I could manage. It was a problem. I wasn't modeling for my children what I wanted to model. Because I couldn't do that, I stopped playing the game. In fact, I deleted all games off my phone completely.

You will be different. Your weakness will be different. You will have to come up with your own solution. Our problems with technology addiction often have to do with some weakness that is unique to us. I don't know what yours is.

Maybe you just can't stop checking your email every time it dings because you love being the office hero and being the one to save the day.

Maybe you are escaping into YouTube as a distraction from work frustrations.

Maybe you can't stop looking at Pinterest and imagining your home as you wish it could be.

Whatever your point of difficulty, find it and set yourself a limit. Part of teaching our children about limits is modeling how to live within limits ourselves. Sometimes the most important limits we can set are around the things that we enjoy the most.

In our next chapter, we are going to tackle the number one, best tool to use to help you set limits for your children and yourself—passwords. Passwords are the doorways to different parts of the digital world, and you need to have a key to every door in your children's world.

Chapter 7

"So that's when I told her, 'I'm not giving you these car keys. I only need them to go from daycare to the playground.'"

Passwords are Doorways

Parents typically have good instincts about how to keep their children safe in the physical world. We keep them in sight. We know when silence means there is a problem. We watch for suspicious people in public spaces. We hold their hands to keep them close in crowded spaces or dangerous areas.

We also work hard to put as many barriers between our family and the dangers of the world as possible. But somehow when it comes to a child's safety in the the digital world, some parents lose their good instincts and don't put up any barriers. All of those things you naturally do to protect your children in the physical world add up to one main thing in the digital world—controlling your child's passwords.

You need to know and control your child's passwords

Passwords are doorways allowing your child access to digital spaces and allowing access to your child for anyone in that digital space. If you do not control your child's passwords, there is no way to control where your child goes, what he sees, who sees her, what he buys, or what she experiences. You are leaving the doors and windows unlocked and wide open.

The Internet as an intersection—hold their hands

Think about it this way. How would you walk with your children across a busy and dangerous intersection? You would hold their hands. Tightly. It wouldn't matter how much those tiny hands squirmed and wanted to walk alone through the traffic, you wouldn't let go. Why? *Because the potential for disaster and tragedy if your children make a small mistake in judgement is life-altering and maybe life threatening.* On the Internet, a small error in judgment can be just as devastating as stumbling into traffic. The Internet is the biggest, most dangerous, fastest, most ridiculous intersection that has ever existed. Any Internet capable device is a gateway to walking across it. Knowing your children's passwords is walking across while holding their hands. Anything less is pushing them into traffic and saying, "good luck, Honey."

But don't they need privacy?

Not when it comes to passwords. Do not be swayed by those who wish to argue that young children have a right to the privacy of their passwords. Children don't need privacy on that scale. Children need to be alone every once in awhile and have some space they feel is theirs, but that is not the same as you not knowing their passwords. You not knowing their passwords means absolute privacy. Do they need that? Absolutely not.

Knowing their passwords has a purpose

Don't forget that you are the parent. You are responsible for controlling the flow of information into their devices, into their minds, and into their hearts. You can't do that without controlling the passwords.

When you don't have their passwords, you don't have access to all the information that your child has access to. You need that access so that you can guide them, help them understand things they are exposed to, and, yes, check up on them.

I have to check up on them?

Children need to learn responsible action. Learning responsible action requires having someone checking up on you. You can't check up on someone who has absolute privacy.

Think about it in the physical world. Don't you look in their rooms to see if they have cleaned up? Don't you check to see if they actually took out the trash? Don't you talk to their teachers to see if they have done their homework? Of course you do all those things. It's the only way for them to learn to be responsible. If your child had absolute privacy, you wouldn't have the access or the ability to check any of those things.

Limited privacy is your children being able to shut the door of their rooms in your house to be alone when they need to be. Children having unlimited control of their own passwords is not like that at all. That is absolute privacy. It's comparable to them living alone, in an apartment, that you aren't allowed to visit, in a city ten times the size of yours. If they aren't old enough to legally live alone, they don't need that kind of privacy.

What's the worst that can happen?

Perhaps some parents are naive enough to believe that the worst that can happen is their children might see some bad pictures or naughty words. But there are real dangers out there in the world, and the Internet is just another doorway for them to enter your home. Any kind of danger can quickly cross digital borders and show up in your real world in costly and scary ways. If you do not know your child's passwords, there is no way to trace what has happened when they get in trouble. If your child goes missing, the answer to what happened could be hidden behind his or her passwords. If your child is a victim of online bullying the evidence could be hidden behind his or her passwords. The worst thing that can happen if you don't know your child's passwords isn't dirty pictures. It is that you may be powerless to help them when something goes wrong.

Once you know the passwords, protect them

You need to protect the passwords better than you are currently protecting your passwords. Because your children already know your passwords.

You are wondering how I can say that? Well, several reasons.

First, most people are really terrible about passwords. So, it's a good guess that your passwords are terrible. Some of your passwords are "password." Some of you use "0000" as your unlock code on your phone, just because it's really fast to type. And most of you probably also use the same password for all your passwords. To get into your bank, your Netflix©, your email, your tax returns or anything else, you use the same password. That's bad. But a lot of us do it. This doesn't just make it easy for criminals to ruin your life, it makes it easy for your children to ruin theirs.

The other reason I know that they know your password is that most children are quicker than you, smarter than you think they are, they see better than you do, and they have a better memory. So guess what. You basically live in a house with tiny superspies, who can see you tap on the screen from across the room and know your unlock code for your phone. They can easily figure out that your password to the computer is their birthday. They watch you and know what code you put in to unlock the Netflix que.

I have personally met children who have their parent's thumbprints on a piece of tape or paper that they use to unlock thumbprint protected devices, like iPhones. Don't underestimate them. Your children are superspies! To stop them, you need to to up your game, get some help, and be vigilant.

An old-school way that still works

One of the best ways to up your game is old-school: use a password protected spreadsheet. Put a password protected spreadsheet on your computer. Choose a good password to protect it, and change that password often! Then enter in all your children's accounts and their passwords. You can keep your passwords in the same document if you want to, or use a different document. This method does require a good bit of work for you to maintain it, but it is simple and doesn't cost anything other than the effort and time you put into it. For an extra level of security, instead of putting the password protected spreadsheet on your computer, put it on a password protected thumbdrive, with a different password, and keep the thumb drive on your keys.

Get help if you need it

The other way is to use an app or password service. There are a lot of very good ones out there. I'd love to recommend one to you here, but the way technology changes, it's probably better for you to check some online reviews and choose one that you think will work the best for you. Remember, you want it to store and keep your passwords safe from your children as well as store and keep their passwords so that you will have access.

Stay vigilant

Once you have the passwords, all you have to do is check in on some kind of schedule. Check at least once a week to make sure that they haven't changed the password to lock you out. Some accounts, such as social media accounts, may have the option of notifying you via email before allowing a password change. Make sure the email for that setting is an email account your children don't have access to and that you will notice when the notification comes in.

You don't have to watch every move they make. Just check in periodically and let them know, that you have been checking in. Do this the way you should be doing everything else in your relationship, by engaging them in conversation. Ask questions about things, give input, and congratulate them on good things you notice. Remember, you aren't spying on them. You are walking with them through a dangerous area, training them to be responsible and aware of their surroundings. Treat this just like any other normal part of your relationship. Your children's passwords should be like their friends. You should know them.

Passwords are just the beginning of keeping your children safe and training them to live with technology. Passwords simply open up devices, files, services, and apps. Once those doors are open, there are many more settings and limits you need to set up. Therefore, when we add technology to our homes, we need to do it in a careful way. That is the subject of our next chapter.

Chapter 8

"I wanted you to have the unboxing experience."

What can I do with the new... ?

When you add something new to your home, it brings a whole series of changes. New technology brings new possibilities. Some of those possibilities are benefits — time savings, new services, access to new information, or new capabilities. But some of those possibilities include new dangers as well.

New Hardware - Opt in to parental controls

Getting new technology ready for your children.

New stuff is awesome. Everyone loves getting new stuff. And one of the top things we love about new stuff is unwrapping it and starting to use it for the very first time. There is even a bizarre industry of people doing "unboxing" videos for new technology products — oohing and ahhing over the sleekness of packaging and the presentation of the items inside.

However, if you are in the United States, when you add new hardware to your home, it will not be ready for your children to use it right out of the box. Every new item will have unique parental controls that have to be activated first. That is because in the United States, we are automatically opted-in for mature content in most cases. In many places around the world, mature content is automatically opted-out, often at a service provider level. That means that in those countries, when you sign up for Internet service or buy new technology, mature content is automatically blocked and you have to opt-in to access mature content. In the United States, that is not the case. Everything you buy will automatically be open to any and all content. If you want to restrict access to mature content, you need to opt-out of it via the parental controls built in to the technology. That's why, before you give your children the new tablet or the new game system, or any new technology item, you need to setup the parental controls ahead of time.

Yes, this does mean that you need to open it first. Open the box, cut open the packaging, turn the device on, read the instructions about setting up the parental controls, adjust the settings, and set the passwords. Depending on the device, it can take awhile, so don't try to do this five minutes before your child's birthday party. Give yourself plenty of time to play with it, learn the controls, and familiarize yourself with the settings—especially if it is a device you have never used before. Then, make sure it is completely charged up, put it back in the packaging, tape it up, wrap it up, and give it to your child.

Your child won't get the "unboxing" experience. But that is a minor pleasure compared to opening it up and it being instantly ready for them to jump on and start playing. Imagine yourself coming in to see your presents on Christmas morning. Would you be happy to see a box full of steel tubing, nuts, bolts, gears, handlebars, and wheels? Or would you prefer to see a fully assembled bike, ready to be ridden, including the training wheels?

New technology hardware comes with "some assembly required." If you give your daughter an iPod touch right out of the box, she'll get to open it, but then you'll just have to take it away for a couple hours to set up all the controls. That's not a happy solution. Your children won't care much that a box has been opened or the packaging is not perfect. When they realize that you took the time to set something up for them so that they can use it immediately, they will love you for it. Opening up fully charged, ready to use technology is way more fun than opening a box with all the manufacturer's seals still in place.

New Software - "Buy" one, get one

Adding apps one at a time

Adding a new piece of hardware isn't the end. New functionality and possibilities are opened with every single app or piece of software that you allow your children to install on their devices. If you open the floodgates and let them add whatever they want, whenever they want, you are going to run into trouble.

Instead, go slowly. Choose carefully. Add one app at a time and learn each new app along with them. Once they have demonstrated they are trustworthy with the one, they can add one more. They may protest, but remember that their excuses are just that: excuses.

Remember your purpose — you are training them to be independent. You have to work with them, show them, and teach them how and why to use each app. This is true of almost any app, but it is doubly true about social media.

Social Media

For the sake of this discussion, let's just assume that your children are over thirteen. (Because even the social networks don't want them on there until they are over thirteen, so why would you let them on there sooner?) If you are going to let them join a social media platform, choose carefully which one to let them join. Consider the different strengths of the platforms, how many friends are using each one, and what the purpose is for the platform. Then join the platform together.

Understand how it functions.

Social networks have similarities and differences. They aren't all alike. You and your child need to explore and learn how the network you choose works. How do you choose who you are connected to? How do I control who sees my posts? How do I see my friends' posts? Does this reveal my location and how do I control that? Can I edit a post? Can I delete one? How do I block spam accounts or accounts sharing inappropriate content? Understanding all of these features takes some getting used to and some investigation. Use the question, "can you teach me?"

What is its purpose?

Every social network has a purpose for why it exists or a question that it is asking. Participation in the social network means trying to answer that question and contribute to the purpose of the network. Use the question, "What do you think about...?"

Build trust and learn responsibility.

Just like they do in any other area of life, children need to build trust that they understand what to do and what not to do. They need to show responsibility in the way they use the new platform. On any social network (or even just with texting) you can't hold your children responsible for what someone else sends, or shares to them, or comments, but you can hold them responsible for how they respond.

Children build trust in this area just like they would when learning to drive a car. They start as a learner and you have to do it with them. Next they prove through guided experience that they have gained a level of skill and competence. Then, they prove that they can be trusted to continue to operate the vehicle without you present. That's how learning something works. Finally, once they complete this cycle, you can consider what new app or platform they want to add.

You will learn about each other as you learn about the apps.

Use the platform you choose to explore their interests. Most social media platforms have search features that let you follow leaders in certain topics. Does your child like space exploration? Tennis? Dance? Great! Help your children find leaders in those areas to follow. You should follow those leaders too.

You should have an account on any platform your children do. You should follow your children and anyone your children follow. You shouldn't comment or react to everything your children do, but you should be one of their connections. Watch who they follow and who follows them. It won't be long before they follow someone that they probably shouldn't follow or some other questionable activity shows up. When that happens, don't freak out. Have a conversation about it. Use the question, "Did you see...?"

When you move into social media alongside your children, it is simply a way to continue growing your relationship as you model appropriate behavior for them.

Gaming and chat

While talking about apps, we also need to talk about an often forgotten or ignored aspect of gaming: chat. Just about every game has some kind of chat or messaging feature. Whether your children play games on phones, tablets, handheld game systems, consoles, or computers, they are probably playing a game with a chat feature. Games of all levels, those for very young children and those with mature content, all have chat. Chat, however, is not rated at all. It is open communication and whoever is on there can say anything that they want. Some games' chat features include direct private messaging between players. The most common problems to pop up on gaming chat will be abusive language and bullying, but there is also the possibility of being enticed to meet up with someone IRL (in real life). You can imagine the myriad dangers possible in that scenario, the least harmful of which is an online fight becoming a real world fight.

Most chat functions in games (and on social media as well) have some method of reporting offensive or dangerous chat behavior and methods of blocking users who engage in this behavior, but you have to know about that behavior in order to teach your child to report such individuals and to block them. This is another reason to learn and use one app at a time and explore apps with your children. Remember, it's not the technology that makes the bullies and abusers. Bullies and abusers are already out there and your children could run into them in a hundred different scenarios. The relationship that you build with your children, the questions you ask and the conversations you invest in are the things that will make the difference in how your children can deal with these situations.

Whenever your children meet bullies or people of an abusive nature, whether online or "IRL," it is an opportunity for conversations about how we treat others, how to forgive, and how to live in a world where people may try to hurt us. Dealing with bullies and difficult people is something your children must learn to do in every aspect of their lives. You wouldn't let them learn about this without any help in real life. Don't leave them alone in the digital world either.

Just, no...

Some apps, you should just say "no" to...

There are definitely some apps you just need to avoid. If we were talking in person, I'd give you a list of apps to avoid and watch out for, but any list I put here will quickly grow less and less useful as more apps are published each day.

So, instead of giving you a list that will be nearly instantly outdated, I'm going to recommend a website to help you keep current on what is out there now. I'll also tell four dangerous features to watch out for that will tip you off to a potentially bad app.

iparent.tv

For current info about apps to avoid and also for help in setting up parental controls on current devices, I recommend checking in regularly at iparent.tv. They do a great job of keeping parents up to date with the latest info about shady apps and things to avoid.

What to ask...

When I am looking at an app I ask the typical adult question and the child question that we talked about earlier in the book. I ask "What will it do for me?" and "What can it do?"

I also ask if this app is setup to help me do, either online or in real life, things I shouldn't be doing. There are four types of features that, as a rule of thumb, are a tip off of an app that is slanted toward illicit purposes. If an app has any of these four features, skip it.

Concealment

Any app that has the purpose of helping you conceal things is bad. Specifically there are several apps to help you hide other apps. Most of these function by making a hidden folder on the device that can only be accessed through the app that installed it. Users hide suspicious apps in the hidden folder so that at a glance it doesn't look like there is anything on the device that shouldn't be there.

Anonymity

If an app is promising anonymity, it usually isn't for a good reason. Also, if you read the EULA (End User License Agreement), you'll notice that the app can't really promise to keep your data anonymous. Location data, user id, device type, phone numbers, emails, and other data is collected and can easily be exposed by hackers. Data can also change hands if the company is sold or goes out of business and another company buys the data for it's own use. But none of that has to happen for this feature to cause trouble. A lot of trouble, embarrassment, and pain can come about when someone figures out your child is the one who "anonymously" asked a really embarrassing question or revealed something embarrassing.

Location-based "chatting"

A key feature that gives away an app usually used for illicit meetings is location-based chatting. If an app allows you to view people who are online nearby and choose to chat or not with them, there is not much good that can come of it.

Disappearing messages or photos

You almost certainly want to avoid any app promising to make communication untraceable or invisible. Apps where messages, photos, or videos "disappear" after being seen, are usually not places where healthy messages of encouragement are shared. Bullying, sexting, and verbal abuse are common among teens on these platforms. Also, as with the promised "anonymity" in other apps, no picture, text, or video sent between devices is ever truly gone. Nothing on the web disappears. It can be captured on the other person's device as a screenshot and then shared publically, or it can be hacked or inadvertently released from the company's servers.

Technology isn't risk free because the world isn't risk free. Even with the most vigilant parents the world isn't worry free and children can still get hurt through technology. In our last chapter, we will look at how to spot the signs that something is going wrong.

Chapter 9

"As long as he stays inside the fence we built, I don't worry about what's going on."

Put Out A BOLO

If you watch police procedurals (and if you watch television at all, it's hard to escape them) you have probably heard this acronym—BOLO. It's one of those bits of jargon that washes over us and we kind of get what it means from context, but many people don't know what it actually stands for—be on look out. As a parent, you aren't on the lookout for dangerous suspects, but for changes that can indicate that there is a problem to investigate.

There are two main areas to watch for changes. One is relational—looking for changes in the behavior of your children and family members. One is technical—looking for changes in settings, usage, and data that affect your family.

Relational markers—Online affects "offline"

People often behave in massively different ways in the online world than they do in real life. Some of the meekest, most polite children face to face can be the meanest, most ruthless bullies online. However, just because they behave differently in one place than another, doesn't mean that problems in one won't affect the other.

As far as your children are concerned, the online world and the real world are merged. They don't experience them as separate places and though their behavior may be different, the emotional effects will carry over from one to the other and cause noticeable changes.

Know your family

My hope for you is that you know your family members well. You have to know them well in order to know when something is wrong. If you aren't well attuned to what is normal, you won't be able to spot fluctuating signals.

Changes

At the most basic level, you are looking for changes. Below is a list of some areas to watch. Sudden changes in these areas are warning signs that something is going on.

- ☐ Moods/Emotional outbursts
- ☐ School performance
- ☐ Behavior problems
- ☐ Obsession with secrecy/privacy
- ☐ Shutting down/not participating in school or family activities anymore
- ☐ Appetite changes

Allies

A BOLO is a call for help from allies in law enforcement. You can't be everywhere your child goes or see your child in every situation. You need to have some allies to help you spot some of these signs. Most of us aren't with our children all the time and, even if you are, you need an outside perspective to see things you might miss. Here is a list of some common allies who may be able to give you valuable information about your children's lives.

- ☐ Relatives
- ☐ School teachers or administrators
- ☐ Church workers
- ☐ Church small group leaders
- ☐ Coaches
- ☐ Tutors
- ☐ Instructors in dance, music, or the arts.
- ☐ Spouses (Including ex-spouses and their new spouses.)
- ☐ Friends (Both your friends and your children's friends.)

Check in with your allies regularly. Have conversations and ask questions about your children.

What have you seen in my children that...was interesting... surprised you...scared you...made you laugh...?
What's the craziest thing...my children are doing...you've heard...you've seen...? Can you teach me how...?

You need to listen proactively to people who interact with your children and learn from their perspective. Sometimes you learn more about your children from their behavior when you are not around than when you are. Invest in having a good relationship and regular communication with these allies. This gives you another window into your children's world and will multiply your chances of getting an early warning of problems in their lives.

Technical Markers—monitoring the data

It is very helpful to monitor and check in on some usage data that can help you spot that there might be an issue with the use of technology. Here are a few areas that you can check periodically on your own. You can use a service or hardware to monitor some of these areas for you.

Data usage—If data usage has a huge spike, more than normal, you know that a big change has happened in how much information is coming into your home. What is causing that spike in data? Music? Movies? Pictures?

Internet browsing history—You should check your browsing history periodically. (If you are using a browser that users log in to, such as Chrome, then you will need to log in as your children to check theirs.) If you notice that a day or week of browser history is deleted, someone is hiding something.

Network slow downs—Your network can slow down when large amounts of data are being downloaded or uploaded. It can also happen when you have hardware that blocks access to some content (such as the Circle with Disney device or other devices.) When someone is trying to access restricted content, the device will be blocking that access and that can cause your network to slow down.

You can monitor these things on your own or you can find a service or device that will do it for you. I use the Circle with Disney device in our home. It recently flagged some activity that I then had to investigate.

We have a basement apartment in our home that we had rented out to a young intern from a local church. He was a great guy—taking classes and pursuing a career in ministry. I loved that my children had a big brother now, who sort-of lived with us. But after he moved in, I saw some markers, some red flags. My network was dragging way down. When I checked the Circle with Disney device I saw why. It was blocking a BitTorrent server that was running on our network.

If you don't know what that is, it's a file sharing protocol. It allows people to share really large files. It has a lot of legitimate uses, but has also been used for some shady things, like movie piracy and mature content. That's why my Circle with Disney device was set to block access.

I see a marker. Now what?

It all comes back to conversation and relationships. It doesn't matter if you spot a technical marker or a relational marker, the reaction should be the same. Use questions to engage in conversation.

In the situation I just described, I found myself having a conversation with a young man, who's not my child, about Internet usage. I had to talk with him and work out what was going on. (He was using the torrent for something with a school project. Nothing bad.) But I still had to have the conversation.

In the story about my son in the introduction, it was an emotional marker that caused me to ask the right kind of question to my son. The answer to that question led to a conversation that saved my son and my family further damage.

Being on lookout is just the beginning. It's an indicator of a possible problem. The way you find out if there actually is a problem—and the way you solve the problem if one is there—is through questions that lead to conversations that build your relationship.

Conclusion

"Not only are the best things in life free, as it turns out, there's not an app for everything."

Empower Your Relationships to Control
(Don't let it be the other way around)

You can't stop what is happening with technology. It's going to keep advancing. Every year, humans will try to use technology to improve their lives. Therefore, technology will become more and more a part of our lives. However, you can continue to build great relationships with your family members, and allow those relationships to guide your use of technology instead of allowing technology to control your relationships.

Relationships influence everything we do and are part of how we understand and interact with the world. The solutions to the problems we face in our technology driven world aren't chiefly technical. They are relational. Even the technical solutions I've discussed — Circle with Disney, locking down passwords, monitoring network usage, and the rest — aren't solutions that will work alone, without relationship.

Remember...

We control technology through relationships.
Relationships are built with conversations.
Conversations start with questions.

☐   What have you seen lately that...?
☐   What's the craziest thing...?
☐   Can you teach me how...?

You are the parent...

Remembering your identity is important to maintaining any relationship. Remember who you are. You are the parent. You can be a friend, but you aren't a peer or buddy. As the parent, guiding your children, teaching them how to navigate their lives, is your role. Teaching them to navigate the world of technology can be intimidating. It is an ever changing landscape of hardware, software, and new devices. But, no matter what kind of crazy technology comes out between now and the time your children leave your home, the answer to how to guide your family through it is the same. It's about your relationship.

...and you can do it!

☐ You can start asking the right questions to investigate how new technology will affect your family.

☐ You can find out both what new technology will do for you and what it will simply do.

☐ You can ask questions regularly to deepen your relationship with your family.

☐ You can set limits and borders for technology in your home in order to focus your home on relationships and not on technology.

☐ You can learn how to properly use technology in your own life so that you can model for your children how to behave with a phone just as you might model for them how to behave at a fancy dinner party.

☐ You can control the doorways and build trust and responsibility by checking up on your children as they learn how to use new technology and demonstrate that knowledge.

☐ You can be on the lookout for behavior that tips you off to problems that could be occurring in your child's world.

Finally, you can cheer your children on as they reach maturity and leave your home, knowing that they can master the use of technology in their lives, and they won't let technology master them.

CPSIA information can be obtained
at www.ICGtesting.com
Printed in the USA
FFOW03n2249140318
45704000-46560FF